William Knapp

New Church Melody

Being a set of anthems, Psalms, hymns. In four parts.

William Knapp

New Church Melody
Being a set of anthems, Psalms, hymns. In four parts.

ISBN/EAN: 9783337042646

Printed in Europe, USA, Canada, Australia, Japan

Cover: Foto ©Lupo / pixelio.de

More available books at **www.hansebooks.com**

NEW CHURCH MELODY:

BEING A SET OF

ANTHEMS, PSALMS, HYMNS, &c.

ON VARIOUS OCCASIONS.

IN

FOUR PARTS.

WITH

A great Variety of other ANTHEMS, PSALMS, HYMNS, &c. composed after a Method entirely new, and never printed before.

By WILLIAM KNAPP,

Author of the first Book of Psalm Tunes and Anthems on various Occasions.

WITH

An Anthem on *Psalm* cxxvii. by one of the greatest Masters in *Europe*. Together with four excellent Hymns, and an Anthem for the Nativity.

I will give thee Thanks in the great Congregation, I will praise thee among much People, Psalm xxxv. 18. *And all her Streets shall say Alleluia,* Tobit xiii. 18.

To which is added,

An Imploration to the KING OF KINGS.

Wrote by King CHARLES I. during his Captivity in *Carisbrook* Castle, in the *Isle of Wight*, Anno Dom. 1648.

Together with

An Anthem for the MARTYRDOM of that blessed PRINCE.

THE FOURTH EDITION

LONDON:

Printed for R BALDWIN, and S. CROWDER and Co. in Pater-noster-Row; the AUTHOR at Poole; B. COLLINS, Bookseller, in Salisbury; and sold by most Booksellers in Great-Britain and Ireland. Price 3s. 6d.
M DCC LXI.

ADVERTISEMENT.

READER,

I HAVE followed the same Rule as in my first Book, by drawing the Work all out in Score, and setting the Tenor in the G. Cliff, the Cantus or Treble stands the upper Part. Some of the Anthems and Psalm-Tunes are not entirely my own Composition, *viz.* the 16th and 139th Anthems: but I was desired by some Friends to compose Counters to them, and publish them with my own Works: Likewise the Anthem taken out of the Communion Service is not my own.

Mr. *Christopher Simpson* in the Preface to his *Compendium of Music*, says, That he hopes it is no Theft to make Use of one's own; I am of that great Man's Opinion, and shall make use of the same Paragraph for a Conclusion, as I did in my Preface to the second Edition of my first Book, it being entirely my own.

If by what I here offer to the Publick, I find I shall be instrumental in propagating the Knowledge of this excellent Art, it will give me a very sensible Pleasure: and with a secret Complacency of Mind, I shall reflect on what I have done, to advance the Praise and Glory of that GOD who is the Author of Harmony.

I hope, therefore, this second Book will be as candidly received as the first, from,

READER,

Your most humble Servant,

William Knapp.

To all Lovers not only of Psalmody, but likewise of Hymns, Spiritual Songs, ond Anthems, and all Harmonious Ways of celebrating the Divine Praises.

BRETHREN,

DIVINE Music commenc'd with the Creation, and, in succeeding Ages, has been honoured with Signals of Divine Approbation. The *Israelites* sang in the Wilderness, and the Water-Spring opened; the Priests and *Levites* sang Praise in the Temple, and the Glory of the Lord filled the House. *Jehosaphat* marched his Army singing, and returned triumphant, his Enemies having slain one another. In the Infancy of the *Christian* Church, *Paul* and *Silas* sung at Midnight in Prison, the Foundations shook, the Prison Doors opened, the Prisoners Bands were loosed, and the Jailor was converted. Here, (says an ingenious Remarker) were Songs in the Night without a *Furia*, and Stones moved by Music without a Fiction.

A worthy Divine, (Dr. BRAY) amongst his other pious Endeavours, has express'd no small Zeal and Skill in recommending and promoting this religious Exercise; and assures us, " That through the Fondness of People for
" Psalm-singing many have recovered their Reading,
" which they had almost forgot, and many have learned
" to read for the sake of singing Psalms:" To this we may add the Testimony of a worthy Minister, written to the Reverend Dr. *Woodward:* " When I first came to
" my Parish, I found to my great Grief, the People very
" ignorant and irreligious; the Place of divine Worship
" indecently kept; the public Service neither understood
" nor attended; the Ministration of the Lord's Supper
" supported only by the Piety of three or four Communicants, and the divine Ordinance of singing Psalms
" almost

"almost laid aside. Now in order to redress this general Neglect of Religion, I began to teach three or four Youths the Skill of singing Psalms orderly, and according to Rules, which greatly tended, through the Grace of God, to awaken their Affections towards Religion, and to give them a Relish for it. The Improvement of these in Psalm-singing being soon observed by others, many young Men desired to be admitted to the same Instruction; which being granted, and the Number of them encreasing daily, they readily submitted to the Rules of a religious Society, and have ever since been careful Observers of them; by whose Means a general Reviving of Piety, and a solemn Observance of the publick Ordinances of God, hath been produced amongst us: And to the Joy of all pious Souls, our Shepherds, Ploughmen, and other Labourers at their Work, perfume the Air with the melodious singing of a Psalm or Hymn to their Creator and Redeemer."

What Daughter of Devotion has so noble an Appearance as this Cælestial * Beauty? For while

*Prayer, as for Alms, does at the Portal wait,
Praise enters, like a Royal Guest, in State.*

When is it that our noble Frequenters of the Almighty's Courts make the greatest Figures, petitioning for Favours, or presenting their Oblations of Respect and Honour? For whoso offers Praise honours him, *Psalm* l. *ult.* With what Elevation of Spirit does the Psalmist start from the Vale of Tears and Supplication, to the Paradise of Praise! The Daughters of the Temple are all of heavenly Race, *Omnes Cælicolæ*, but not *Omnes supera alta tenentes*: The *Fastigia Cæli* are the Prerogative of Psalmody. How different is the Stile of their Addresses! Be merciful to me for I have sinned, says Penitence! From

---

* I shall make no Apology for mentioning Psalmody as a Princess and Beauty, as *Solomon* speaks of Wisdom, *Plato* of Virtue, Classick Poets of the Graces; nor for not confining her to the single Province of Psalm-singing, but likewise including Hymns, Spiritual Songs, Anthems, and all harmonious Ways of celebrating the divine Praises.

the Ends of the Earth, and out of the Deep have I cried, says Prayer: O be joyful in the Lord, come before his Presence with a Song, &c. This is the Language of Praise.

Accordingly some also of our own Poets;
For Prayer the Ocean is, where diversly
Men steer their Course, each to a different Coast,
Where oft our Int'rests so discordant be,
That half beg Winds, by which the rest are lost.
Sir W. D.

But Praise is Devotion fit for mighty Minds; the differing World's agreeing Sacrifice, *&c.* nor only the common Sacrifice of Rational Beings; but so just a Tribute to the Almighty, that inferior Creatures, Elements, and the whole Universe, are summon'd to pay it, *Psalm* 148.

And for its being Devotion fit for mighty Minds, if you doubt a Poet's Word, take a Preacher's. "Singing the "Praises of God is the noblest Part of Worship, the "most generous Service that we can perform, and car- "ries with it the liveliest Signatures of a divine and God- "like Temper of Mind." Thus the practical Discourser, and what can a Poet say more? But still this Preference to other religious Duties must be understood in some certain Respects, not in every Respect. And we acknowledge each of the fair Competitors to be a Princess and Sovereign in her own Province: Yet Psalmody, in her sublimest Exercise, (that of celebrating the divine Attributes and Perfections) appears with the Grandeur of an Empress.

In sacred Heraldry she has the Ascendant, as being of the eldest House, and early as the Creation, when the Morning Stars sung together; and of a Lineage that will last when Time shall be extinct.

For when to the Cælestial Temple come,
Petition there shall cease, and Pray'r be dumb:
But Praise, in Accents more sublime and strong,
Shall then commence her everlasting Song.
W. K.

TO
Mr. KNAPP,
ON HIS NEW
CHURCH MELODY.

IS it the justest Praise of every Art,
To second Nature, and improve the Heart?
Then sure amidst the Circle none can vie
With true Devotion's Handmaid, *Psalmody*.

When meditating all that's good and great,
The Soul sinks down beneath the mighty Weight
Of the divine Perfections, what shall ease
The lab'ring Thought, but Strains divine as these?

But various Passions act the human Mind,
To Joy, to Grief, to Pray'r, to Praise inclin'd:
When our rude untaught Tongues would these express,
What but a Godlike Art can find the Dress?

How great your Merit, who employ your Pains
To form the Choir, to regulate its Strains!
And shewing Musick why herself was given,
Recall the Wand'rer to her native Heaven!

AN ALPHABETICAL TABLE,

For the more readily finding any ANTHEM, HYMN, or PSALM, contained in this Book.

B.

	Page
BRING unto the Lord, &c. an Anthem, Pfalm 29.	39
Behold how good and joyful, &c. an Anthem, Pfalm 133.	64
Behold that Splendor, &c. a Carol.	162
Bleffed be the Lord God, an Anthem, Luke 1.	172

E.

Except the Lord, an Anthem, Pfalm 127.	79

G.

Glory be to God on high, an Anthem in the Communion Service.	88
Great Monarch, &c. King Charles I.	182

H.

Hear O Heavens, &c. an Anthem, Ifaiah 1.	11
How bleft is he who ne'er confents, Pfalm 1.	107

I.

I will fing, &c. an Anthem, Exodus 15.	32
I faid I will take heed, an Anthem, Pfalm 39.	94
Inftruct me in thy Statutes, Lord, Charlton Tune, Pfalm 119.	155
Juft Judge of Heaven, &c. Langton Tune, Pfalm 43.	123

L.

Lord hear the Voice, &c. Ham-Prefton Tune, Pfalm 5.	109
Let all the Lands, &c. Corfe-Caftle Tune, Pfalm 66.	132

M.

Moft gracious God, &c. an Hymn.	1
My Lot is fall'n, &c. Pfalm 16.	54
My Life's a Shade, my Days, &c. a Funeral Hymn.	105

My

An Alphabetical Table, &c.

	Page
My Heart is set, &c. Psalm 57.	130

O.

O God thou hast been displeased, &c. an Anthem, Psalm 60.	3
O Praise the Lord, &c. an Anthem, Psalm 147, &c.	19
O Lord thou hast searched me out, &c. an Anthem, Psalm 139	48
O all ye People, &c. Worth Tune, Psalm 47.	125
O be joyful, &c. an Anthem, Psalm 100.	70
O Sight of Anguish, &c. a Carol.	168
Of Mercy's never failing Spring, &c. Keynson Tune, Psalm 101.	141
O God my Heart is fully bent, &c. Knighton Tune, Psalm 108.	146
O pray we then for Salem's Peace, &c. Clapper Tune, Psalm 122.	149
O Praise the Lord with one Consent, &c. Corfe-Mullen Tune, Psalm 135.	151

S.

Since I have placed, &c. Creekmore Tune, Psalm 11.	114
Sing ye with Praise, &c. Wimborne Tune, Psalm 96.	136
Sing to the Lord, &c. Ham-Worthy Tune, Psalm 98.	138

T.

To celebrate thy Praise, &c. Long-Ham Tune, Psalm 9.	112
The Lord to thy Request, &c. Long Fleet Tune, Psalm 20.	116
The King, O Lord, &c. Sandwich New Tune.	119
To God in whom I trust, &c. Studland Tune, Psalm 25.	121
The Lord hath spoke, &c. Knowl Tune, Psalm 50.	127
To bless thy chosen Race, &c. Keynson Tune, Psalm 67.	134
They that in Ships, &c. Poole New Tune, Psalm 107.	144
To God the mighty Lord, &c. Canford Tune, Psalm 136.	153
Thou Lord by strictest Search, &c. Blandford Tune, Psalm 139.	157
Th' Eternal speaks, &c. a Carol.	164
The Beauty of Israel is slain, an Anthem, Sam. 2. Chap. 1.	187

W.

While Shepherds watched, the Angel's Hymn.	159

A Hymn

Lord hear my pray'r accept my Song,
And sanctify my mind;
And grant I may my whole life long,
Be Virtuously inclin'd.

That when thou may'st my Soul require
And I must hence remove;
I then may join the Heav'nly Choir,
And sing with Saints above.

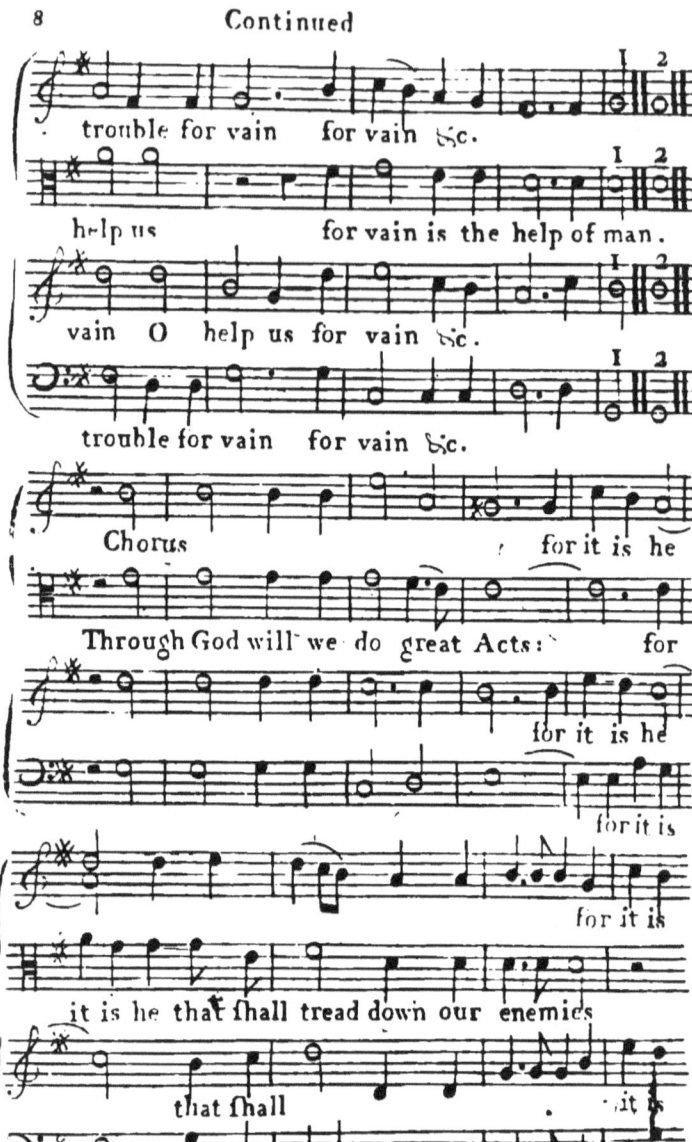

An Anthem Pſalm 147ᵗʰ. Ver. 1ˢᵗ for the reeſta_
bliſhment of Peace or any other time A 4 Voc.

End with the first Strain and Chorus and the Amens and Hallelujahs or with the Chorus Great is our L. &c. and the Amens and Hallelujahs as follows

Continued

An Anthem Exodus 15th For a thanksgiving for a Victory or at any other time. A 4. Voc.

Continued

An Anthem Pfalm 29th
A 4 Voc.

it is the Lord that commandeth the waters it is the glo - - - rious God that maketh the thunder

Sing the Chorus again
Ascribe unto the Lord &c.

Verse Counter

It is the Lord that ruleth the Sea the voice of the Lord is mighty in operation the voice of the Lord is a glo - - - rious voice y voice of the Lord is a

Sing the Chorus again
Ascribe unto the Lord &c.

glorious voice.

Verse Bass

. The voice of the Lord the voice of the Lord divi - - - deth divi - - - deth the fla - - - mes of fire

Verse Counter

The voice of the Lord sha - - - - keth the wilderness

Continued

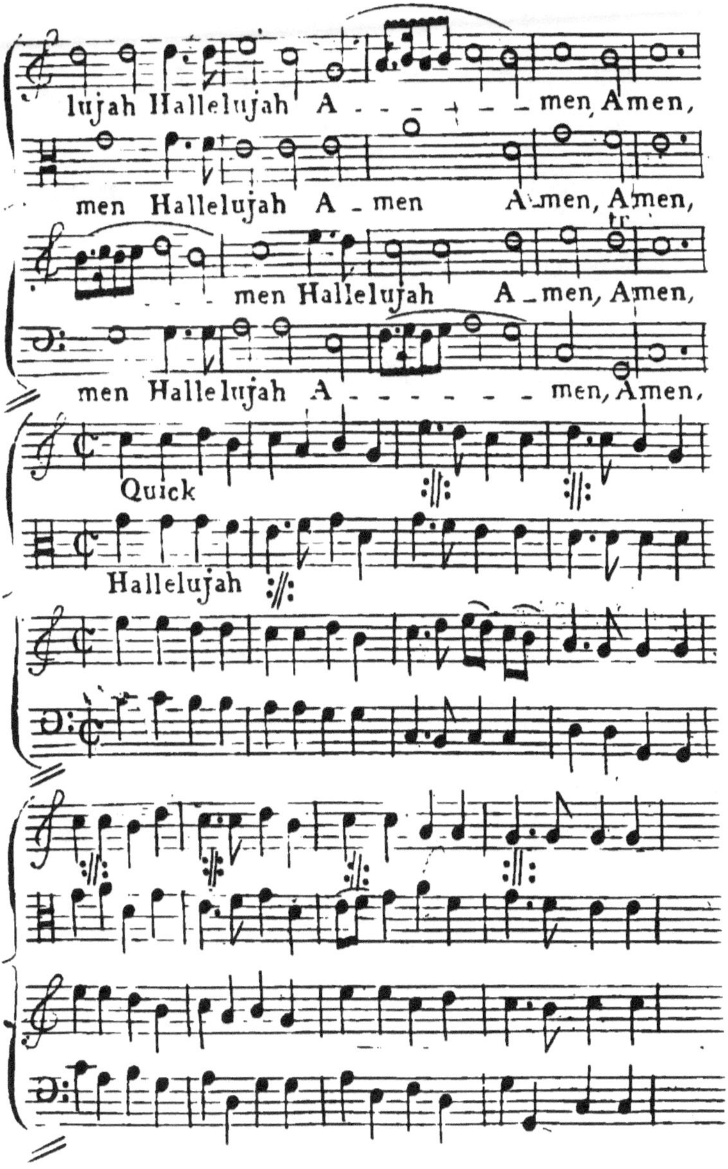
lujah Hallelujah A - - - - - - men, Amen,
men Hallelujah A - men A - men, Amen,
tr
- - - men Hallelujah A - men, Amen,
men Hallelujah A - - - - - - - men, Amen,
Quick
Hallelujah

An Anthem Psalm 139th
A 3 Voc.

Continued

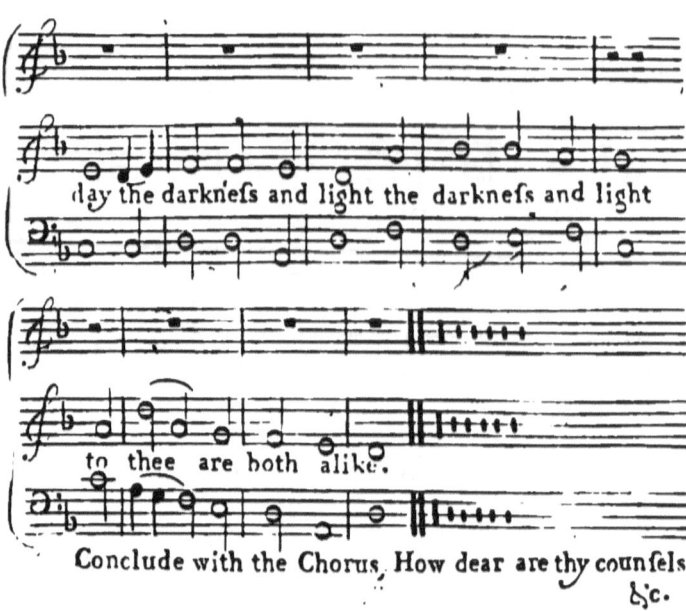

day the darkness and light the darkness and light to thee are both alike.

Conclude with the Chorus, How dear are thy counsels &c.

Psalm 19th Verse 5th New Version A.3.Voc.

My lot is fall'n in that bless'd Land, where
My lot is fall'n in that bless'd

Continued

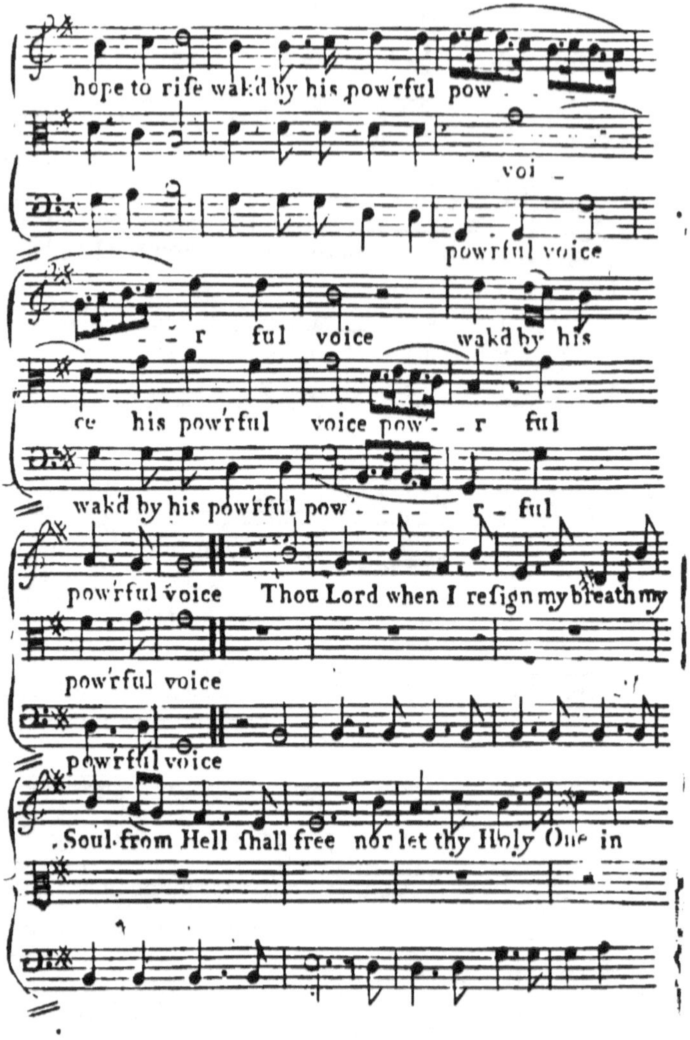
hope to rise wak'd by his pow'rful pow - - -
voi -
pow'rful voice
- - - r ful voice wak'd by his
ce his pow'rful voice pow' - - r ful
wak'd by his pow'rful pow' - - - - r - ful
pow'rful voice Thou Lord when I resign my breath my
pow'rful voice
pow'rful voice
Soul from Hell shall free nor let thy Holy One in

Continued

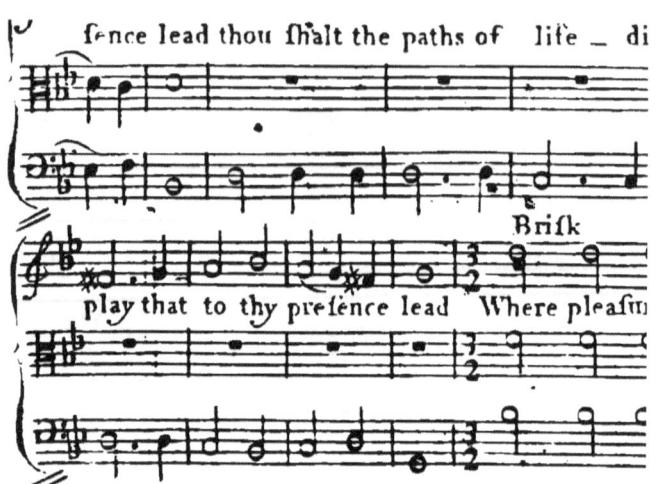

66   Continued

ran down unto the beard: even unto *Aarons*

ran down &c.

and went down to the skirts of his cloth_

beard   and went down to the skirts

and went down

ing

of his clothing

to the skirts of his clothing clothing

and went down and went down to the skirts of his

Continued

Chorus … of his cloth-ing … Like as the clothing clothing dew of Hermon, like as the dew of Hermon of Hermon which fell upon the hill of Sion, For

An Anthem Pſalm 100th
by Mr H. Brown.   A 4 Voc.

Continued

71

Continued

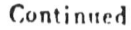

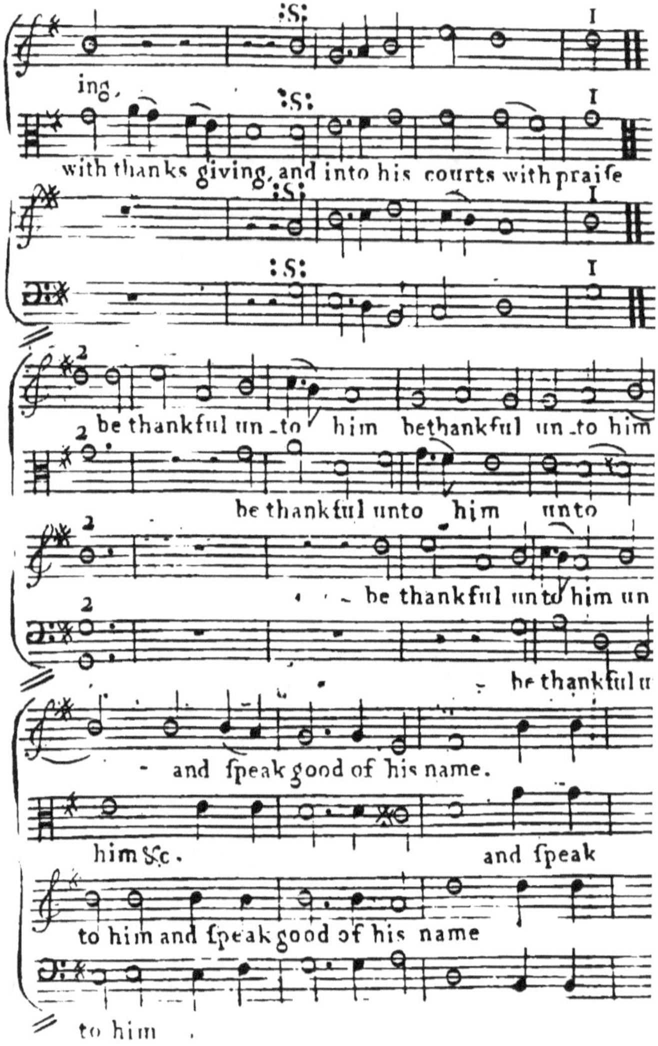
:S:
I
ing,
:S:
I
with thanks giving, and into his courts with praise
:S:
I
:S:
I
2
be thankful un-to him bethankful un-to him
2
be thankful unto him unto
2
be thankful unto him un
2
be thankful u
and speak good of his name.
him &c.
and speak
to him and speak good of his name
to him

Continued

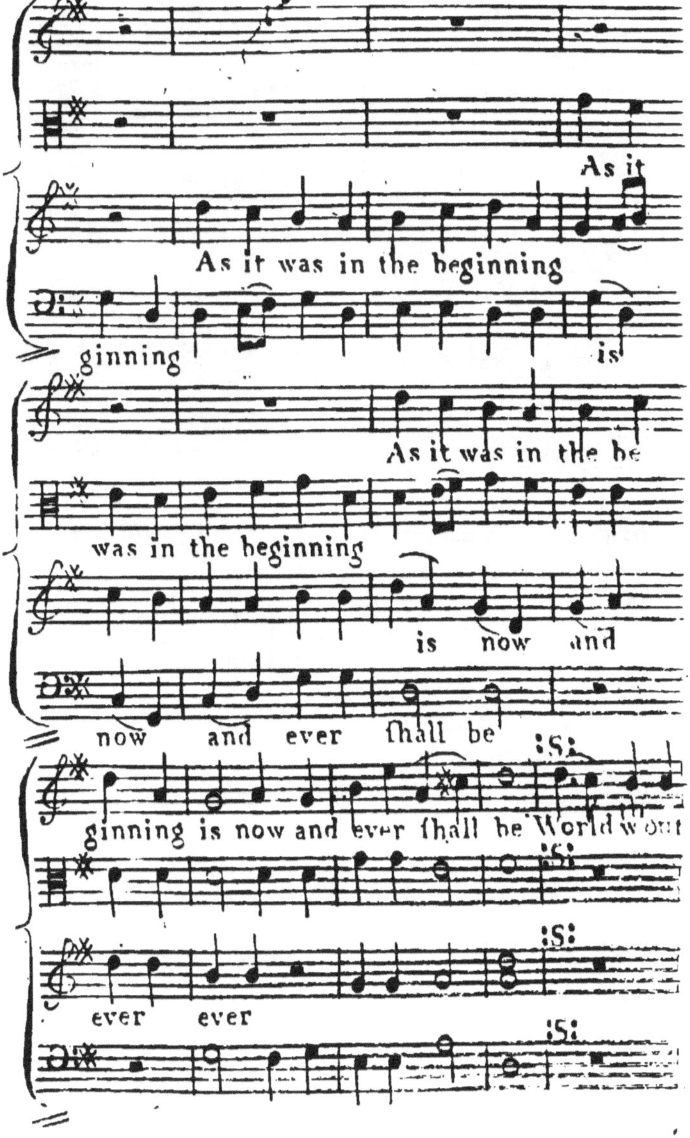
As it
As it was in the beginning
ginning
is
As it was in the be
was in the beginning
is now and
now and ever ſhall be
:S:
ginning is now and ever ſhall be World w out
:S:
:S:
ever ever
:S:

An Anthem Psalm 127.th A 3. Voc.

Continued

Continued

Continued

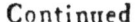

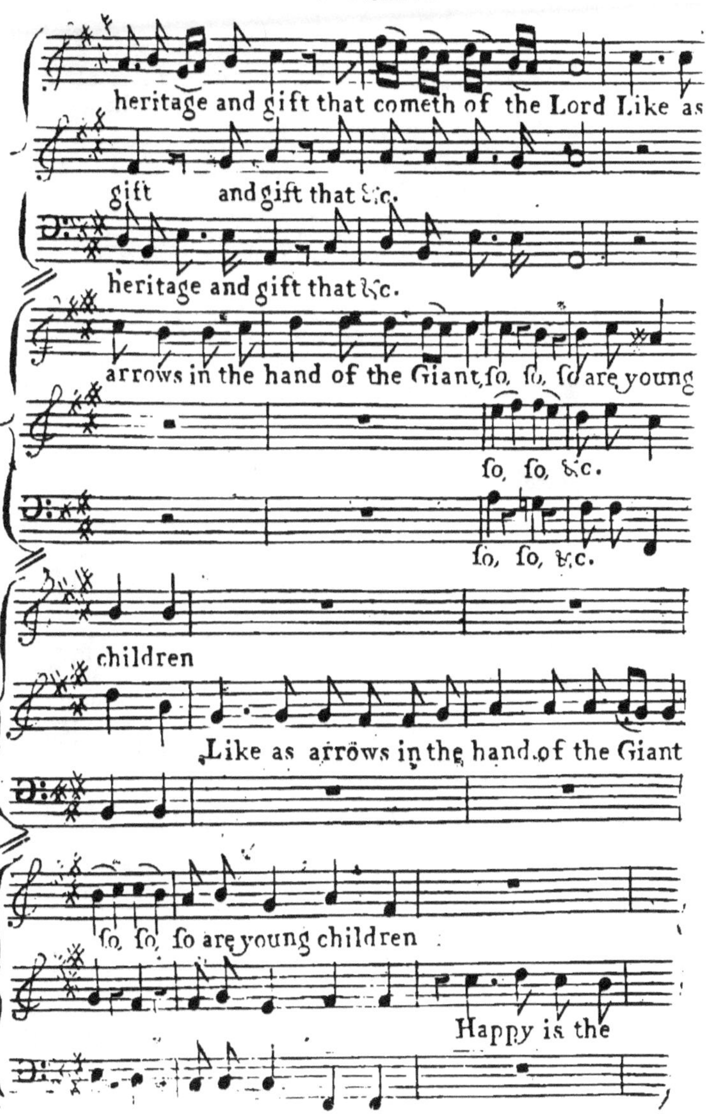
heritage and gift that cometh of the Lord Like as
gift and gift that &c.
heritage and gift that &c.
arrows in the hand of the Giant so, so, so are young
so, so, &c.
so, so, &c.
children
Like as arrows in the hand of the Giant
so, so, so are young children
Happy is the

Continued

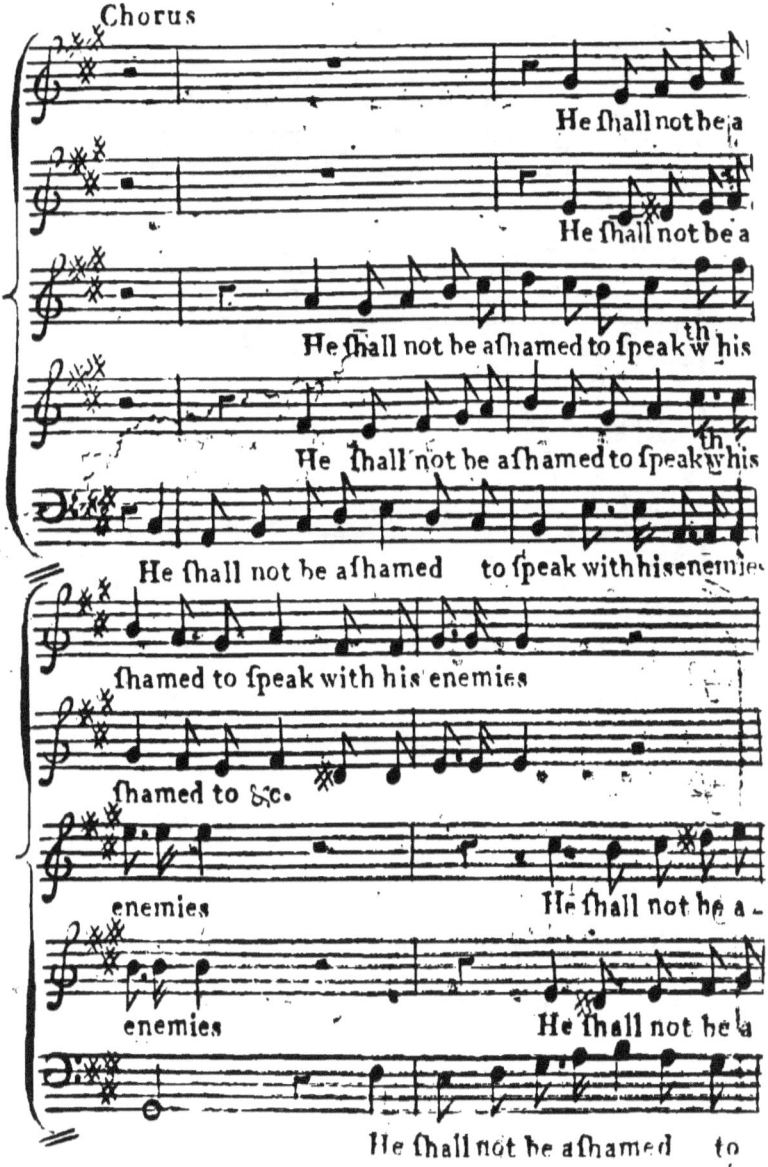

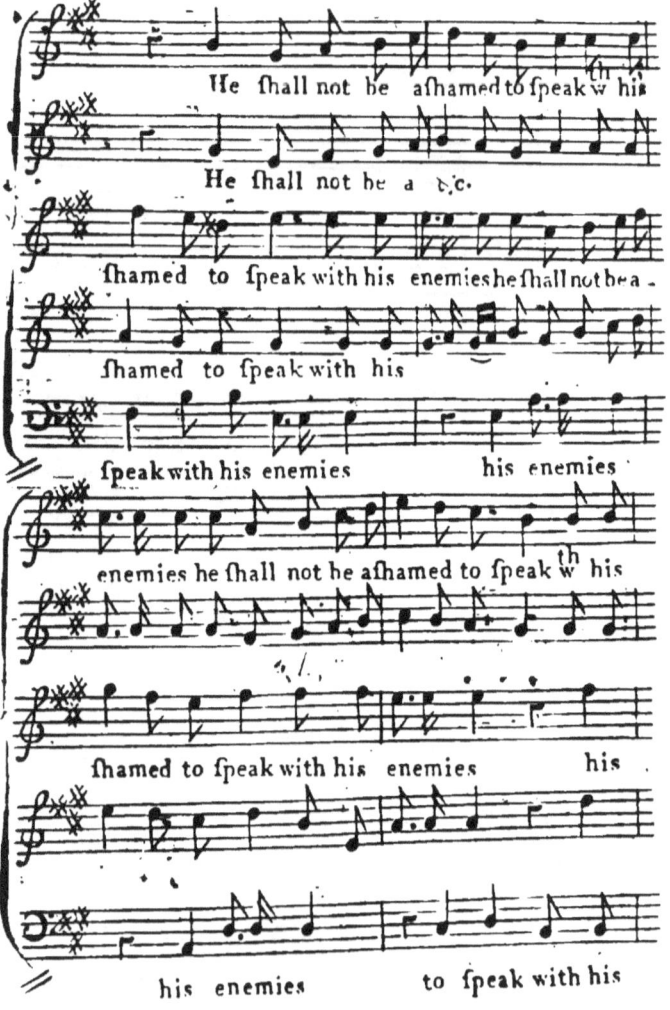

88 An Anthem taken out of the Communion Service A 3 Voc.

Glory be to God on
Glory be to God on high,
and in earth peace,

high, and in earth peace,
good will towards men
and in earth peace, good will towards

good will towards men to God on high,
and in earth peace Glory be to God on high,
men

and in earth peace good will towards men we praise thee
we

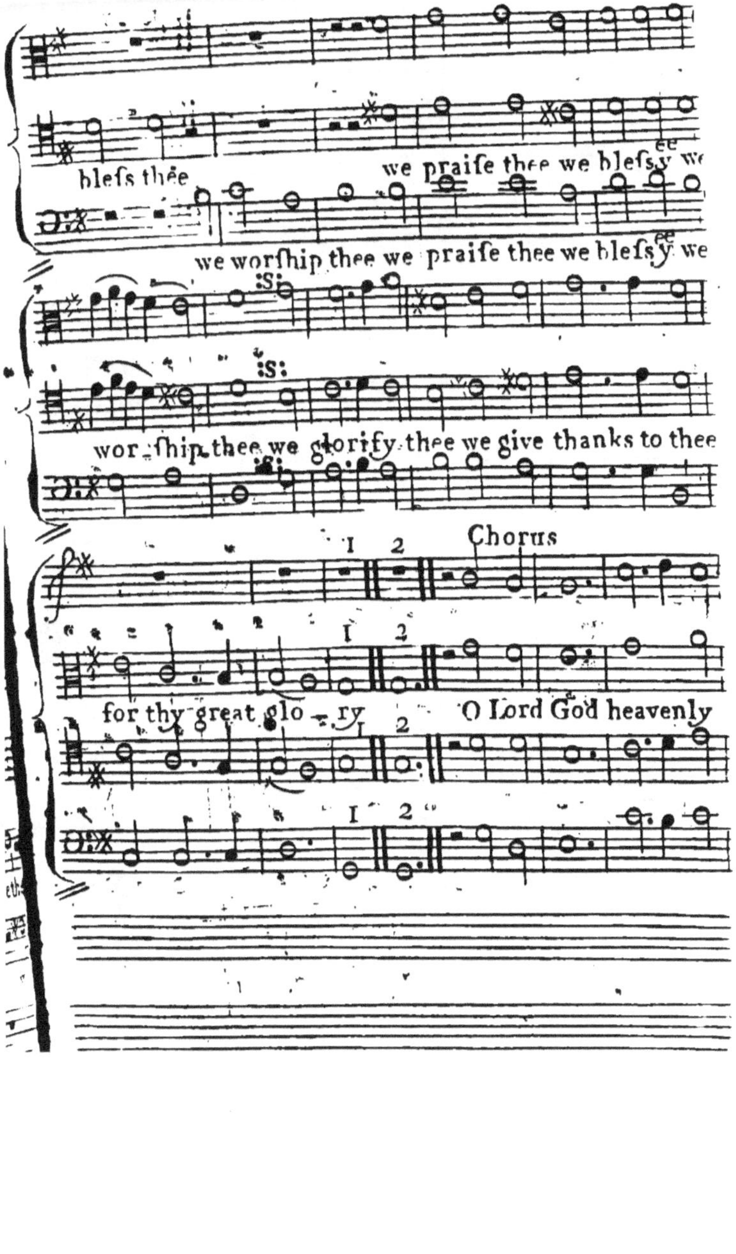
blefs thee we praife thee we blefs yee we
we worfhip thee we praife thee we blefs yee we
:S:
:S:
wor-fhip thee we glorify thee we give thanks to thee
1 2
Chorus
1 2
for thy great glo - ry
2
O Lord God heavenly
1 2

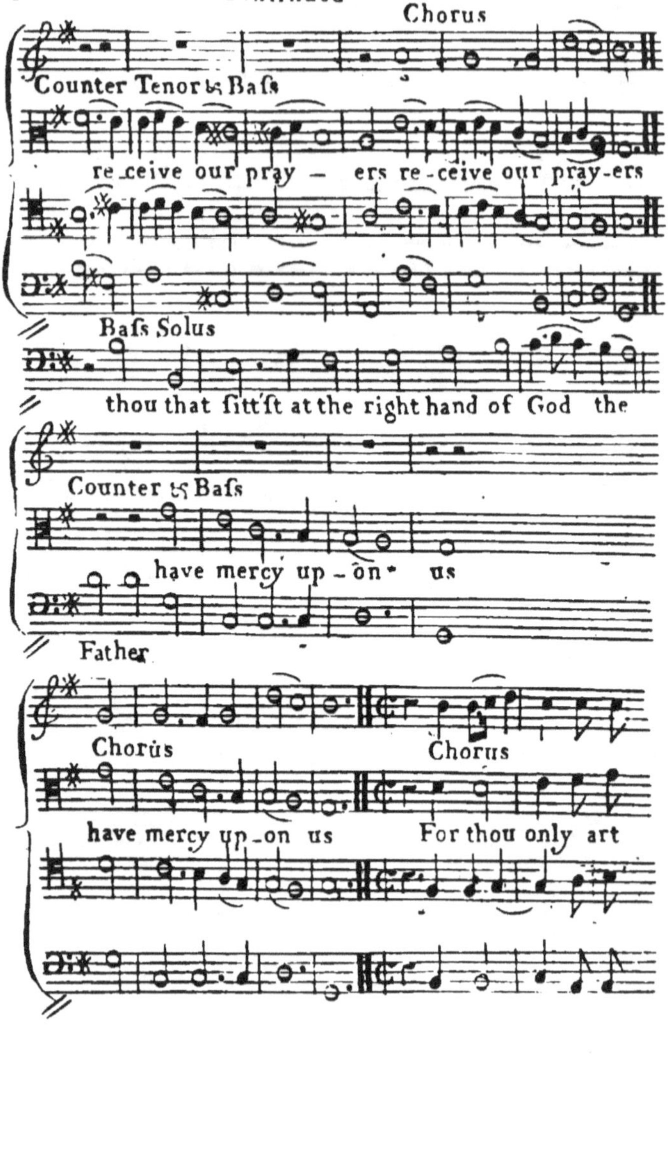
Chorus
Counter Tenor & Bass
re-ceive our pray - ers re-ceive our pray-ers
Bass Solus
thou that sitt'st at the right hand of God the
Counter & Bass
have mercy up-on us
Father
Chorus
Chorus
have mercy up-on us
For thou only art

94   Continued

God the Father in the glory of ... of God the
ther in the glory of God the
God the Father in the glory of God of
Fa - ther in the &c.

Father A — men
Father A — men

An Anthem Pſalm 39.th A 4 Voc.

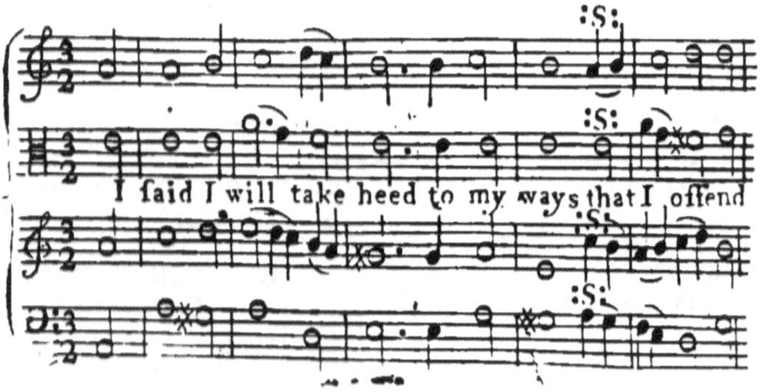

I ſaid I will take heed to my ways that I offend

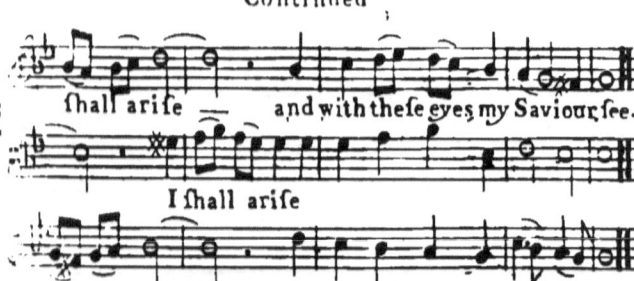

My peaceful grave shall keep My bones till y^e sweet day,
I wake from my long sleep, And leave my Bed of Clay.
                          Sweet truth &c.

My Lord his Angels shall Their golden Trumpets sound,
At whose most welcome call My grave shall be unbound.
                          Sweet truth &c.

I said sometimes with tears, A me! I'm loath to die.
Lord, silence thou those fears, My life's with thee on high.
                          Sweet truth &c.

What means my trembling heart, To be thus shy of death;
My life and I shan't part, Tho' I resign my breath.
                          Sweet truth &c.

Then welcome harmless grave, By thee to Heav'n I'll go,
My Lord his death shall save Me from the Flames below.
                          Sweet truth &c.

Parkston Tune Psalm 1st. New Ver. A 4 Voc.

Continued.

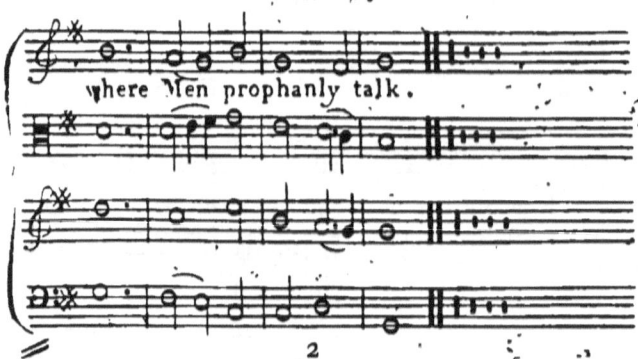

where Men prophanly talk.

2
But makes the perfect Law of God
   His Business and Delight;
Devoutly reads therein by Day,
   And meditates by Night.

3
Like some fair Tree, which fed by streams
   With timely Fruit does bend,
He still shall flourish, and Success
   All his Designs attend.

4.
Ungodly Men and their Attempts
   No lasting Root shall find;
Untimely blasted, and dispers'd
   Like Chaff before the Wind.

5
Their Guilt shall strike the Wicked dumb
   Before their Judge's Face:
No formal Hypocrite shall then
   Amongst the Saints have place.

Continued.

For God approves the Juſt Man's Ways,
   To Happineſs they tend:
But Sinners and the Paths they tread
   Shall both in Ruin end.

Ham-Preſton Tune Pſalm 5th. New Ver. A 4 Voc.

Lord hear the voice of my Complaint,

Lord hear y^e voice of my Com-

Lord hear the

of my Com —

plaint, of my Com —

voice of my Complaint, com —

Lord hear the voice of my Com —

Continued.

3

Thou in the morn my Voice shalt hear;
   And with the dawning day
To thee devoutly I'll look up,
   To thee devoutly pray.

4

For thou the Wrongs that I sustain
   Canst never, Lord, approve,
Who from thy sacred Dwelling place
   All Evil dost remove.

6

The sland'ring Tongue, O God of Truth,
   By thee shall be destroy'd,
Who hat'st alike the Man in Blood
   And in Deceit employ'd.

7

But when thy boundless Grace shall me
   To thy lov'd Courts restore,
On thee I'll fix my longing Eyes,
   And humbly thee adore.

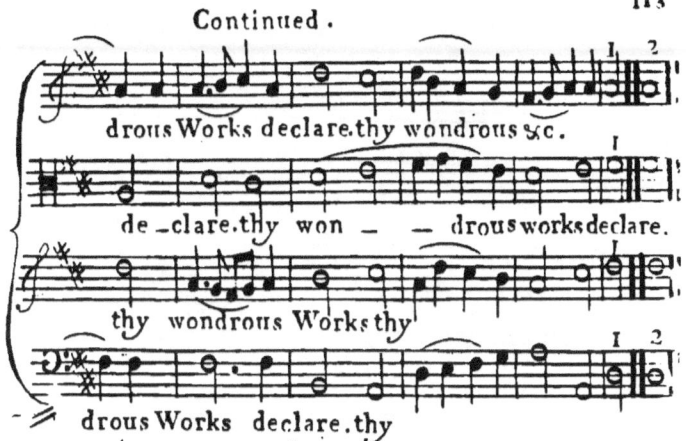

N^B. If this Tune is Sung for a Thanksgiving for a Victory Sing y^e 4. 1st Verses of y^e Psalm.

2

The Thought of them shall to my Soul
    Exalted Pleasure bring,
Whilst to thy Name, O thou most High!
    Triumphant Praise I sing.

10

All those who have his Goodness prov'd
    Will in his Truth confide;
Whose Mercy ne'er forsook the Man
    That on his Help rely'd.

11

Sing Praises therefore to the Lord,
    From *Sion* his Abode
Proclaim his Deeds, till all the World
    Confess no other God.

Creekmoor Tune Psalm 11th New Ver. A 4 Voc.

Continued.

2
Behold, the wicked bend their Bow,
  And ready fix their Dart;
Lurking in ambush to destroy
  The Man of upright Heart.

3
When once the firm Assurance fails
  Which publick Faith imparts,
'Tis time for Innocence to fly
  From such deceitful Arts.

4
The Lord has both a Temple here,
  And righteous Throne above;
Whence he surveys the Sons of Men,
  And how their Counsels move.

The righteous Lord will righteous Deeds,
  With signal Favour grace;
And to the upright Man diclose
  The brightness of his Face.

Long-Fleet Tune Psalm 20th New Ver. A 4 Voc.
For a publick Fast in time of War.

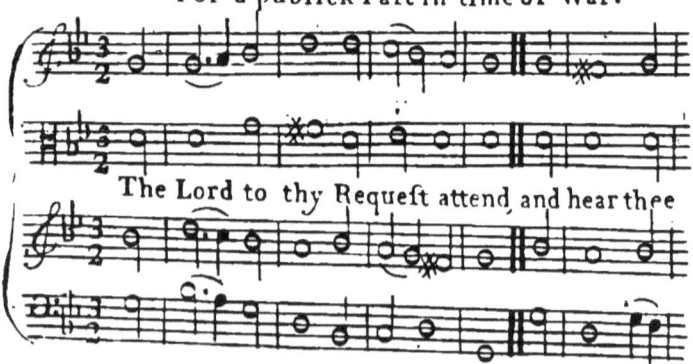

The Lord to thy Request attend and hear thee

Continued.

Continued

2
To aid thee from on high repair,
    And ſtrength from *Sion* give;
Remember all thy Offrings there,
    Thy Sacrifice receive.

3
To compaſs thy own Heart's Deſire
    Thy Counſels ſtill direct;
Make kindly all Events conſpire
    To bring them to effect.

4
To thy Salvation, Lord, for Aid
    We chearfully repair,
With Banners in thy Name diſplay'd:
    The Lord accept thy Pray'r.

5
Our Hopes are fix'd, that now the Lord
    Our Sov'reign will defend,
From Heav'n reſiſtleſs Aid afford,
    And to his Pray'r attend.

6
Some truſt in Steeds for War deſign'd,
    On Chariots ſome rely;
Againſt them all we call to mind
    The Pow'r of God moſt High.

For thou whate'er his Lips requeſt
Not only doſt impart,
But haſt with thy Acceptance bleſt
The wiſhes of his Heart.

3

Thy Goodneſs and thy tender Care
Have all his Hopes out-gone;
A Crown of Gold thou mad'ſt him wear,
And ſet'ſt it firmly on.

He pray'd for Life and thou, O Lord,
Didſt to his Pray'r attend,
And graciouſly to him afford
A Life that ne'er ſhall end.

3
Those who on Thee rely
Let no disgrace attend.
Be that the shameful Lot of such
As wilfully offend.

4   5
To me thy Truth impart,
And lead me in thy way,

Continued

For thou art he that brings me Help,
On thee I wait all day.

6

Thy Mercies and thy Love,
O Lord recall to mind;
And gracioufly continue ftill,
As thou wert ever, kind.

7

Let all my youthful Crimes
Be blotted out by thee;
And for thy wond'rous Goodnefs fake
In Mercy think on me.

8

His Mercy and his Truth
The righteous Lord difplays,
In bringing wand'ring Sinners home,
And teaching them his ways.

Langton Tune   Pfalm 43^d New Ver. A 4 Voc.
Canon two parts in one

Juft Judge of Heav'n, againft my Foes do

Juft Judge of Heav'n, againft my Foes do

Continued

2

Since thou art still my only Stay,
  Why leav'st thou me in deep Distress?
Why go I mourning all the Day,
  Whilst me insulting Foes oppress?

3

Let me with Light and Truth be blest,
  Be these my Guides, to lead the way,
Till on thy holy Hill I rest,
  And in thy sacred Temple pray.

Continued

4

Then will I there fresh Altars raise,
 To God, who is my only Joy;
And well-tun'd Harps with Songs of Praise
 Shall all my grateful Hours employ.

5

Why then cast down, my Soul, and why
 So much oppreft with anxious Care?
On God, thy God, for Aid rely,
 Who will thy ruin'd State repair.

Worth Tune Pfalm 47th. New Ver. A 4 Voc.

O all ye People clap your Hands, and with triumphant Voices fing. No force the mighty Power w

Continued

stands, Of God the Universal King.

stands, Of God the Universal King.

     3 4
He shall opposing Nations quell,
  And with Success our Battles fight;
Shall fix the Place where we must dwell,
  The Pride of *Jacob,* his delight..
     5 6
God is gone up, our Lord and King,
  With Shouts of Joy and Trumpets Sound;
To him repeated Praises sing;
  And let the chearful Song go round.
     7 8
Your utmost Skill in Praise be shown,
  For him who all the World commands;
Who sits upon his righteous Throne,
  And spreads his Sway o'er Heathen Lands.

        9
Our Chiefts and Tribes, that far from hence
  To serve the God of *Abr'am* came,
Found him their constant sure Defence.
  How great and glorious is his Name!.

A low Bass to the Chorus which might be Sung by two or three deep Voices together with the four upper Parts.

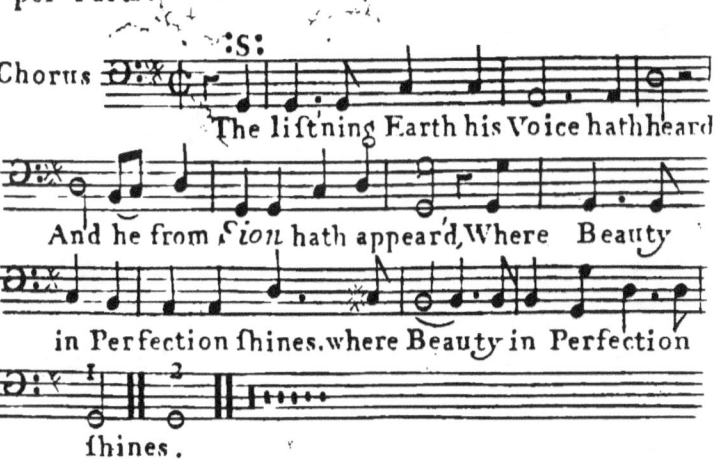

Chorus: The lift'ning Earth his Voice hath heard, And he from Sion hath appear'd, Where Beauty in Perfection shines, where Beauty in Perfection shines.

3. 4.

Our God shall come, and keep no more
Misconstru'd silince as before,
But wasting Flames before him send:
Around shall Tempests fiercely rage,
While he does Heav'n and Earth engage
His just Tribunal to attend.

5. 6.

Assemble all my Saints to me
(Thus runs the great Divine Decree)
That in my lasting Cov'nant live,
And Off'rings bring with constant Care,
(The Heav'ns his Justice shall declare,
For God himself shall Sentence give.)

Awake my joy, awake, I say,
My Lute, my Harp, and string:
And I my Self before the day,
Will rise, rejoyce, and sing.

11
Among the People I will tell
The goodness of my God:
And shew his Praise that doth excel
In heathens land abroad.

132   Continued

    His mercy doth extend as far
      As the Heav'ns all are high:
    His truth as high as any Star,
      That shineth in the Sky.

Set forth and shew thy Self, O God,
    Above the Heav'ns most bright:
Exalt thy Self on Earth abroad,
    Thy Majesty and might.

Corfe Castle Tune   Psalm 66 New Ver.   A 4 Voc.

Let all the Lands with shouts of Joy To God their Voices raise. Sing Psalms in Honour of his Sing Psalms in

Continued

Continued

3

And let them say, How dreadful, Lord,
In all thy works art Thou!
To thy great Pow'r thy stubborn Foes
Shall all be forc'd to bow.

4

Thro' all the Earth the Nations round
Shall Thee their God confess;
And with glad Hymns their awful Dread
Of thy great Name express.

5

O come, behold the works of God,
And then with me you'll own,
That he to all the Sons of Men
Has wond'rous Judgments shown.

Kinson Tune Psalm 67th. New Ver. A 3 Voc.

To bless thy chosen Race, In Mercy, Lord, in-cline, And cause the brightness of thy Face On

Continued

all thy Saints to shine.

2

That so thy wond'rous Ways
May thro the World be known;
While distant Lands their Tribute pay,
And thy Salvation own.

3

Let diff'ring Nations join
To celebrate thy Fame;
Let all the World, O Lord, combine
To praise thy glorious Name.

4

O let them shout and sing,
With Joy and pious Mirth,
For Thou, the Righteous Judge and King,
Shalt govern all the Earth.

5

Let diff'ring Nations join
To celebrate thy Fame;
Let all the World, O Lord, combine
To praise thy glorious Name.

136 Winborne Tune Psalm 95th Old Version.

Treble & Tenor.

Sing ye with praise with praise un-to the

Sing ye with praise un-to the

Lord, New Songs with joy with joy and mirth:

Lord, New Songs with joy and mirth:

Counter & Bass.

Sing un-to Him with one with one accord, all

Sing un-to Him with one accord,

People on the Earth the Earth:

all People on the Earth:

Yea, sing unto the Lord alway, Praise ye his

Continued

holy Name: Declare and shew from Day to Day,

Salvation by the same.

9
Fall down and worship ye the Lord
  Within his Temple bright:
Let all the People of the World
  Be fearful at his sight.

10
Tell all the World, be not afraid,
  The Lord doth reign above:
Yea, he the Earth so fast hath stay'd,
  That it can never move.

Continued

11
And that it is the Lord alone
  Who rules with Princely might:
To Judge the Nations ev'ry one
  With Equity and Right.

12
The Heav'ns shall joyfully begin,
  The Earth likewise rejoyce:
The Sea with all that is therein,
  Shall shout and make a noise.

13
The Fields shall Joy and ev'ry thing
  That springeth on the Earth:
The Wood and ev'ry Tree shall sing
  With gladness and with mirth.

14
Before the presence of the Lord,
  And coming of his might:
When he shall justly Judge the World,
  And rule his Folk with right.

Ham Worthy Tune Psalm 98th. New Ver. A 4 Voc.

Continued

2

The Lord has through th'aſtoniſht World
Diſplay'd his ſaving Might,
And made his righteous Acts appear
In all the Heathens ſight.

4

Let therefore Earth's Inhabitance
Their chearful Voices raiſe,
And all with Univerſal Joy
Reſound their Makers praiſe.

5

With Harp and Hymns ſoft Melody.
Into the Conſort bring
The Trumpet and ſhrill Cornets ſound,
Before th'Almighty King.

Keynſon Tune Pſalm 101ſt New Ver. A 4 Voc.
On A King or Queens acceſſion to the Crown

Continued

Continued.

2
When, Lord, thou shalt with me reside,
Wise discipline my Reign shall guide;
With blameless Life my self I'll make
A Pattern for my Court to take.

3 4
No ill Design will I pursue,
Nor those my Fav'rites make that do.
Who to Reproof bears no regard,
Him will I totally discard.

5
The private Slanderer shall be
In publick Justice doom'd by me:
From haughty looks I'll turn aside,
And mortifie the Heart of Pride;

6
But Honesty call'd from her Cell,
In splendor at my Court shall dwell:
Who Virtues practice make their Care,
Shall have the first Preferments there.

7
No Politicks shall recommend
His Countrey's Foe to be my Friend:
None e'er shall to my Favour rise
By flatt'ring or malicious Lyes.

25

No sooner his command is past,
But forth a dreadful Tempest flies,
Which sweeps the Sea with rapid Haste.
And makes the stormy Billows rise:

26

Sometimes the Ships, tos'd up to Heav'n,
On tops of mounting Waves appear,
Then down the steep Abyss are driv'n,
Whilst ev'ry Soul disolves with fear.

27

They reel and stagger to and fro,
Like Men with Fumes of Wine opprest;
Nor do the skilful Seamen know,
Which way to steer, what Course is best.

28

Then strait to God's indulgent Ear
They do their mournful Cry addrefs;
Who graciously vouchsafes to hear,
And frees them from their deep Distress.

Knighton Tune. Psalm 108th. New Ver. A 4 Voc.

Continued 147

Name Shall ce-lebrate thy Fame.

2
Awake, my Lute; nor thou, my Harp,
  Thy warbling Notes delay;
Whilst I with early Hymns of Joy,
  Prevent the dawning Day.

3
To all the list'ning Tribes, O Lord,
  Thy wonders I will tell,
And to those Nations sing thy Praise,
  That round about us dwell:

4
Because thy Mercy's boundless height
  The highest Heav'n transcends;
And far beyond th'aspiring Clouds
  Thy faithful Truth extends.

5
Be thou, O God, exalted high
  Above the starry Frame;
And let the World, with one consent,
  Confess thy glorious Name.

Clapper Tune Pfalm 122d Verfe 6th New Ver. A 4 Voc. 149

For the reeftablifhment of Peace or at any other Time

Continued

God! Who bear true Love to thee.

7

May Peace within thy sacred Walls
  A constant Guest be found,
With Plenty and Prosperity
  Thy Palaces be crown'd.

8

For my dear Brethren's sake, and Friends
  No less then Brethren dear,
I'll pray — May Peace in *Salem's* Tow'rs
  A constant Guest appear.

9

But most of all I'll seek thy Good,
  And ever wish thee well,
For *Sion* and the Temple's sake,
  Where God vouchsafes to dwell.

His worthy praiſe proclaim

2

Praiſe him all ye that in his Houſe,
    Attend with conſtant care;
With thoſe that to his outmoſt Courts
    With humble Zeal repair.

3

For this our trueſt Intreſt is
    Glad Hymns of praiſe to ſing;
And, with loud Songs to bleſs his Name,
    A moſt delightful thing.

Gloria Patri

To Father, Son and Holy Ghoſt.
    The God whom we adore,
Be Glory: As it was, is now,
    And ſhall be evermore.

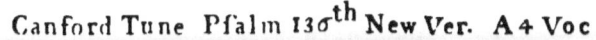

Canford Tune Psalm 130th New Ver. A 4 Voc

Continued

To him whose wond'rous Pow'r
All other Gods obey,
Whom earthly Kings adore,
This grateful Homage pay:
   For God, &c.

By his Almighty Hand
Amazing Works are wrought;
The Heav'ns by his Command

155

Continued

Were to perfection brought.
For God, &c.

He spread the Ocean round,
About the spacious Land;
And made the rising Ground
Above the Waters stand.
For God, &c.

25 26
He does the Food supply
On which all Creatures live:
To God who reigns on high
Eternal Praises give.

For God will prove
Our constant Friend,
His boundless Love
Shall never end.

Charlton Tune Psalm 119th Verse 33d New Ver. A 4 Voc

Instruct me in thy Statutes Lord Thy righteous

Instruct me in thy Statutes Lord Thy righteous

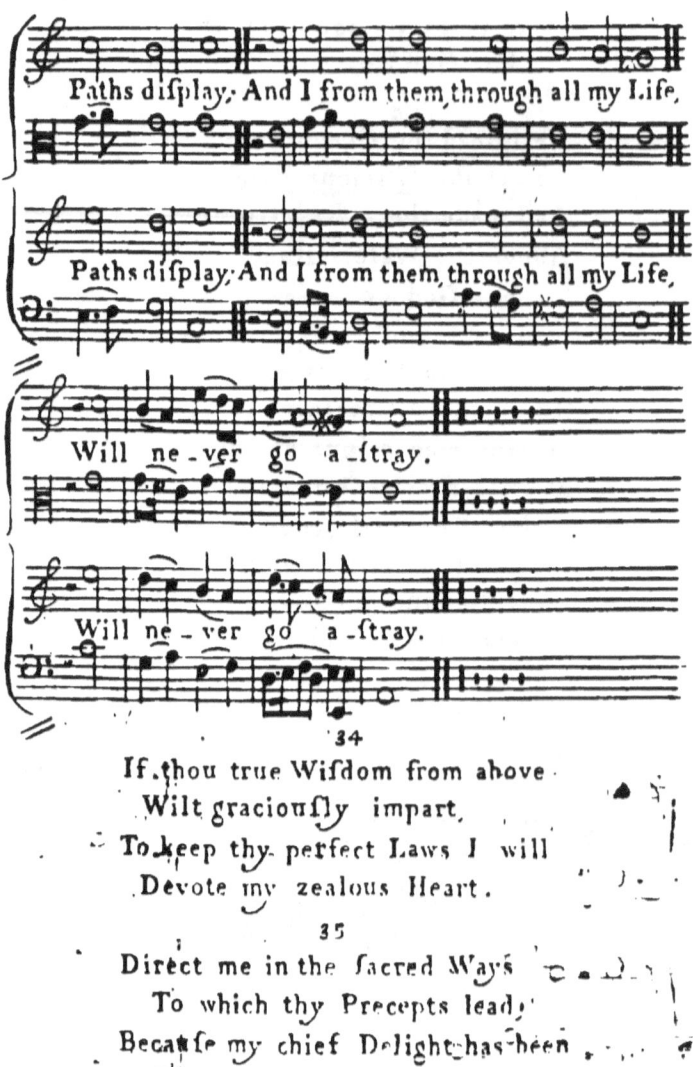

34

If thou true Wisdom from above
Wilt graciously impart,
To keep thy perfect Laws I will
Devote my zealous Heart.

35

Direct me in the sacred Ways
To which thy Precepts lead;
Because my chief Delight has been
Thy righteous Paths to tread.

Continued

36

Do thou to thy moſt juſt Commands
Incline my willing Heart;
Let no deſire of worldly Wealth
From thee my Thoughts divert.

The above & ye following Tune are Set in the two Natural Keys Viz: Are the Natural ♭ Key, and Cfaut the Natural ♮ Key, and when Sung, to be repeated every Line.

Blandford Tune Pſalm 139th New Ver. A 4 Voc

Thou Lord, by ſtricteſt ſearch haſt known   My

Thou Lord, by ſtricteſt ſearch haſt known   My

riſing up, and ly-ing down; My ſe-cret Thoughts

riſing up, and ly-ing down; My ſe-cret Thoughts

Continued

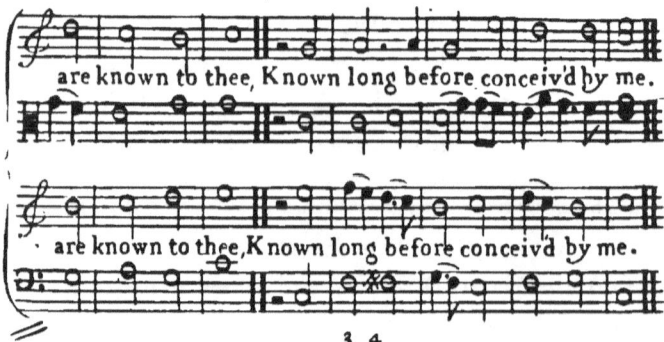

are known to thee, Known long before conceiv'd by me.

are known to thee, Known long before conceiv'd by me.

3 4
Thine Eye my Bed and Path survey
My publick Haunts, and private ways;
Thou know'st what 'tis my Lips would vent,
My yet unutter'd Words intent.

5 6
Surrounded by thy Pow'r I stand,
On every side I find thy Hand
O Skill for human reach too high!
Too dazling bright for mortal Eye!

7
O cou'd I so perfidious be
To think of once deserting thee,
Where, Lord, cou'd I thy Influence shun,
Or whither from thy Presence run!

8
If up to Heav'n I take my flight,
'Tis there thou dwell'st, enthron'd in light:
Or dive to Hell's infernal Plains,
'Tis there Almighty Vengeance reigns.

The End of the Psalms

Here follow four Excellent Hymns and an Anthem for the Nativity

The Song of the Angels, at the Nativity of our Blessed Saviour. St Luke 2^d. Ver 8th A 4 Voc.

While Shepherds watch'd their Flocks by night All seated on the Ground, The Angel of the

Continued

2
Fear not, said he (for mighty Dread
  Had seiz'd their troubled mind)
Glad Tidings of great Joy I bring
  To you, and all Mankind.

3
To you, in *David's* Town, this Day
  Is born of *David's* Line,
The Saviour, who is Christ the Lord;
  And this shall be the Sign:

4
The heav'nly Babe you there shall find
  To human view display'd,
All meanly wrapt in swathing Bands,
  And in a Manger laid.

5
Thus spake the Seraph, and forthwith
  Appear'd a shining Throng
Of Angels praising God, and thus
  Address their Joyful Song:

6
All Glory be to God on high,
  And to the Earth be Peace
Good will, henceforth, from Heav'n to Men,
  Begin and never cease.

W

A Carol, or Redemption the Wonder of Angels. 1749.

A 4 Voc.

Continued

2

Why does the King approach our Land?
Comes he with Thunder in his hand,
　　The Merit of our Crimes?
Shepherds be glad; He comes with Peace,
Not wrath, but Universal Grace,
　　To bless ev'n distant Climes. Shepherds &c.

3

See Heav'ns great Heir a Woman's Son!
Behold, a Manger is his Throne!
　　Nay, see him born to die.
Yours is the Guilt, but his the Pain;
His are the Sorrows, yours the Gain
　　Then let his Praise be high.　Yours be &c.

4

Come mighty King the Grace enhance
A Stable was thy Palace once,
　　Dwell in these Hearts of ours:
Teach us to praise the Father's Love
Till blest, transported, fir'd above,
　　We sing with Nobler Powers.　Teach us &c.

The Counsels of Grace　A Carol 1750 A 5 Voc.

Continued

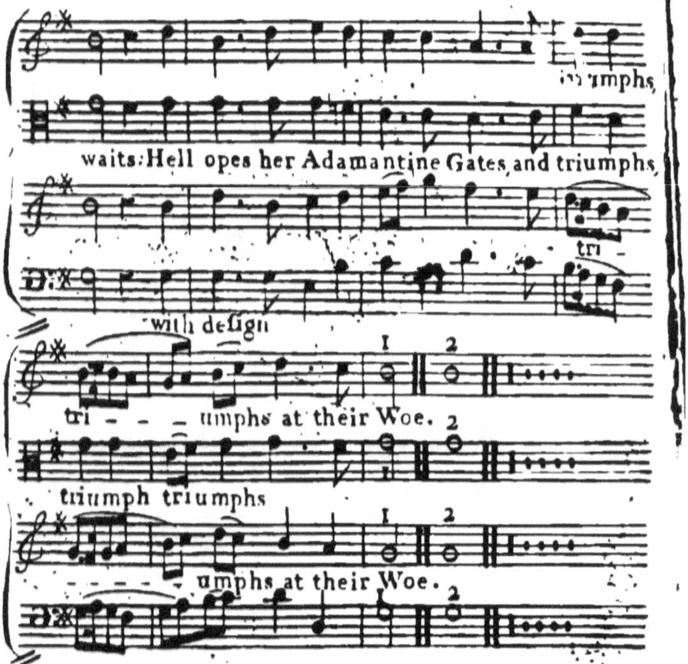
umphs,
waits: Hell opes her Adamantine Gates, and triumphs,
tri -
with design
1 2
tri - - - umphs at their Woe. 2
triumph triumphs
1 2
- - - - - umphs at their Woe. 2

A low Bass to the Chorus which might be Sung by two or three deep Voices, together with the four upper parts.

Chorus

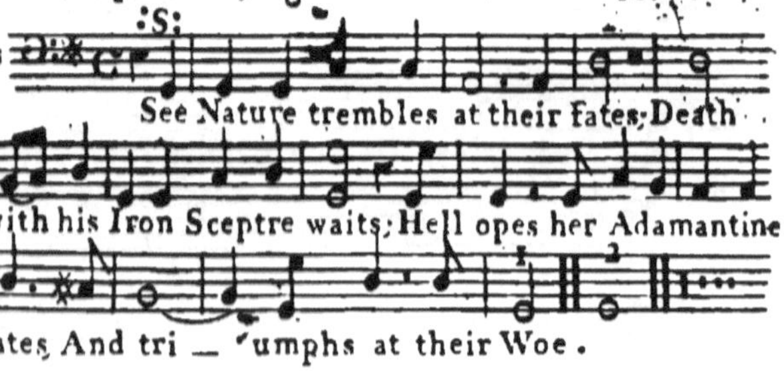
:S:
See Nature trembles at their fates; Death
with his Iron Sceptre waits; Hell opes her Adamantine
1 2
Gates, And tri - umphs at their Woe.

Continued

2
Which of the bright Cæleftial throng,
With Love fo warm and heart fo ftrong,
    Dares Languifh on a Crofs?
Who can leave Liberty for Chains,
Abbandon Extafy for Pains,
What Angel — fortitude fuftains,
    Th'ineftimable Lofs.
Who can leave &c.

3
He faid; and Death=like Silence Reign'd;
Deep was their awe; the radiant band,
    The mighty Tafk declin'd.
At length Heav'ns Prince the filence broke,
And Ardent, thus, the Sire befpoke,
None but thy Son can ward the ftroke;
    Then let the tafk be mine.
At length &c.

4
Mine, be the feeble Infant=State;
Mine, in return for Love, be hate;
    A Manger be my Throne.
Pain, when thy Glory calls is blifs,
When Mans in danger Tortures Peace,
Shame praife, a Paradice th'Abyfs:
    Then yeild thy darling Son.
Pain when thy Glory &c.

Th'Almighty radiance fmil'd Afsent,
Loud was the fhout that *Æther* rent,
    All Heav'n was in amaze.
Go my Lov'd Image, faid the Sire,
Be born in anguifh to expire;
Earth triumph; Angels, ftrike the Lyre
    To Everlafting Praife.
Go my Lov'd Image &c.

- ve him friendly aid.

2
Why do no rapid Thunders roll;
Why do no tempests Rock the Pole?
   O Miracle of Grace!
Or why no Angel on the wing,
Warm for the Honours of their King,
   T'extirpate all the race. Or why no &c.

3
Did he, that Infant bath'd in tears!
Call into form the rolling Spheres;
   Did Seraphs wait his Nod?
Helpless he calls, but Man delays,
The Moral Chaos disobeys
   This offspring of a God. Helpless he &c.

4
Say, radiant Seraphs, thron'd in light,
Did Love e'er tow'r so high a flight,
   Or Glory sink so low?
This wonder Angels scarce declare,
Angels the rapture scarce can bear,
   Or equal praise bestow. This wonder &c.

Continued.

  Redemption! 'tis a boundless Theme!—
  Thou boundless Mind, our hearts inflame
   With ardor from above:
  Words are but faint let joy express;
  Vain is mere joy, let actions bless
   This Prodigy of Love. Words are &c

  Advertisement.

The three last Carols were sent me according as they bare date, by a Gentleman unknown, desiring me to Set them to Music. with the third I received the following Letter. W.K.

 Sir

  I take the liberty, tho' unknown, of troubling you with another Carol which I beg you will do me the Honour of Setting to Music. if this performance as I fear it will, should prove less animated than the occasion requires; your candor must ascribe it, in some measure to an illness under which I have long labour'd, and which has greatly depres'd my Spirits and likewise to the frequency of my attempts upon the same subject, this before you being the fifth Composition of the kind. you will see here too many Symptoms of a Sickly Muse. And yet I expect that Music which works wonders, and is known to be So vereign in some diseases, will at least give her a more sprightly Air, if not totally relieve her. It will not be the first instance, in which Poetry has been supported, enlivend and recommended by the help of her Sister-Art. my own obligations of this sort to yo I take this oppertunity of very Sincerely and than

Continued

fully acknowledging.

Some time or other I may pofsibly make fo free, as to fend you a few Songs in behalf of which I fhall intreat the fame afsiftance from that Art, in which you are fo acknowledged a Mafter. Amufements of that kind, when decently entertaining being, in my apprehenfion, no way difhonourable to the Cloth I wear. Pleafe to return the new Carol afsoon as pofsible and you will lay a double obligation on your Obedient Humble

         Servant &c.

An Anthem for the Nativity S.t Luke the 1.st Ver. the 68.th Or inftead of Jubilate Deo in the Morning Service A 4 Voc.

Continued

173

Continued.

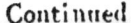

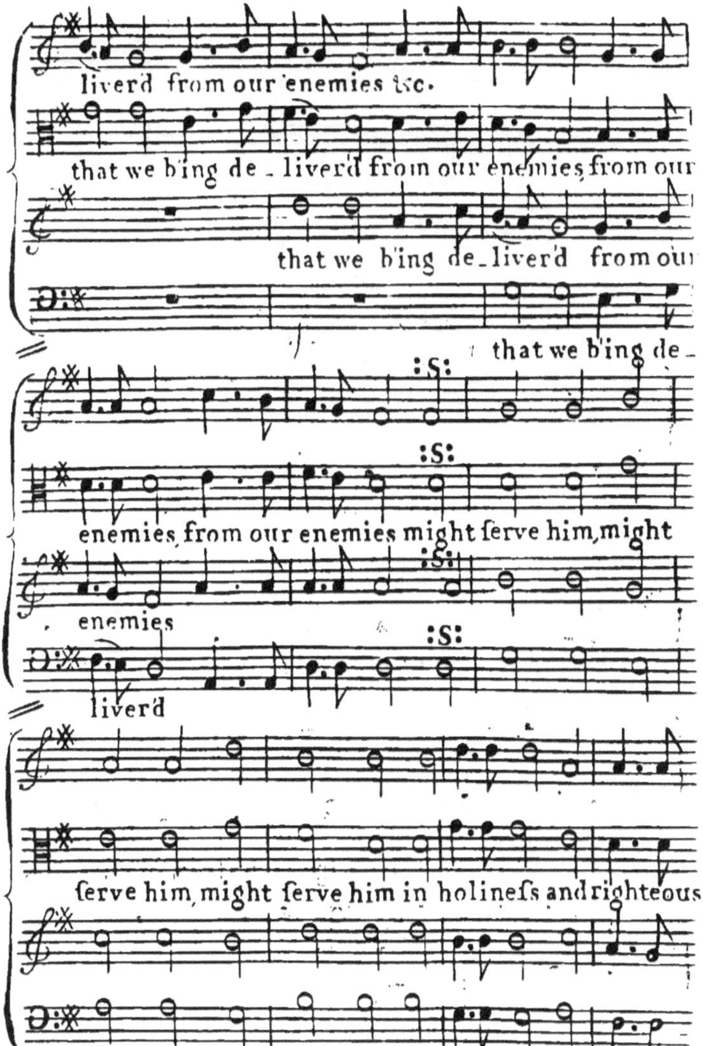
liverd from our enemies &c.
that we bing de - liverd from our enemies from our
that we bing de - liverd from our
that we bing de -
enemies from our enemies might ferve him, might
enemies
liverd
ferve him, might ferve him in holinefs and righteous

KING CHARLES I.

*being Majesty in Misery An Im-
ploration to the King of Kings wrote
by his Majesty during his Captivity in
Carisbrooke Castle Anno Dom 1648
Set to Musick by the Author*

A 3 Voc.

Great Monarch
Great Monarch of the World,
Great Monarch of the World, Great Monarch
of the World, &c. The Poten-
of the World Whence Pow—er springs
of the World Whence Pow—er springs
cy and Pow'r of earthly Kings, Re-
Record the
Record the Roy-

And teach my Tongue, that ever did confine
Its Faculties in Truth's Seraphick Line,
To track the Treason of thy Foes and mine.

Nature and Law, by thy Divine Decree,
The only Root of righteous Royalty
With this dim Diadem invested me;

With it the sacred Sceptre, Purple Robe,
The Holy Unction and the royal Globe,
Yet I am levell'd with the Life of Job.

The fiercest Furies that do daily tread
Upon my Grief, my gray discrowned Head,
Are those that owe my Bounty for their Bread.

They raise a War, and Christen it The Cause,
Whilst Sacrilegious Hands have best Applause
Plunder and Murder are the Nation's Laws.

Tyranny bears the Title of Taxation,
Revenge and Robbery are Reformation,
Oppression gains the Name of Sequestration.

My Loyal Subjects, who in this bad Season,
Attend me by the Law of God and Reason,
They dare impeach, and Punish for High Treason.

Continued

Next at the Clergy do these Furies frown,
Pious Episcopacy must go down;
They will destroy the Crosier and the Crown.

Churchmen are chain'd, and Schismaticks are freed
Mechanicks Preach, and Holy Fathers bleed;
The Crown is crucified with the Creed.

The Church of England doth all Faction foster,
The Pulpit is usurp'd by each Imposter,
Extempore excludes the *Pater Noster*.

The *Presbyter* and *Independant* Seed,
Springs with broad Blades to make Religion bleed
Herod and *Pontius Pilate* are agreed.

The Corner Stone's misplac'd by every Paviour,
With such a Bloody Method and Behaviour,
Their Ancestors did Crucify our Saviour.

My royal Consort, from whose fruitful womb,
So many Princes legally have come,
Is forc'd in Pilgrimage to seek a Tomb.

Great *Britain's* Heir is forced into *France*
Whilst on his Father's head his foes advance;
Poor Child he weeps out his Inheritance.

Z.

With my own Power, my Majesty they wound
In the King's Name the King himselfs uncrown'd.
So doth the dust destroy the Diamond.

With Propositions daily they inchant,
My People's ears, such as do reason daunt,
And the Almighty will not let me grant.

They promise to erect my royal Stem,
To make me great, to advance my Diadem,
If I will but fall down and worship them.

But for refusing they devour my Thrones,
Distress my Children and destroy my Bones,
I fear they'll force me to make Bread of Stones.

My Life they prize at such a slender rate,
That in my Absence they draw Bills of Hate,
To prove the King a Traytor to the State.

Felons obtain more Privilege than I,
They are allow'd to answer ere they die,
'Tis Death for me to ask the reason why.

But Sacred Saviour with thy Words I wooe
Thee to forgive, and not be bitter to,
Such as thou knowest know not what they do.

Continued.

For since they from the Lord are so disjointed,
As to contemn those Edicts he appointed,
How can they prize the power of his anointed.

Augment my Patience, nullifie my Hate,
Preserve my Issue and inspire my Mate,
Yet though I perish, bless this Church and State.

An Anthem Sam. 2d Chap. 1st Ver. 19th A 4 Voc
For the Martyrdom of King Charles the First
or at any other Time

190

Continued

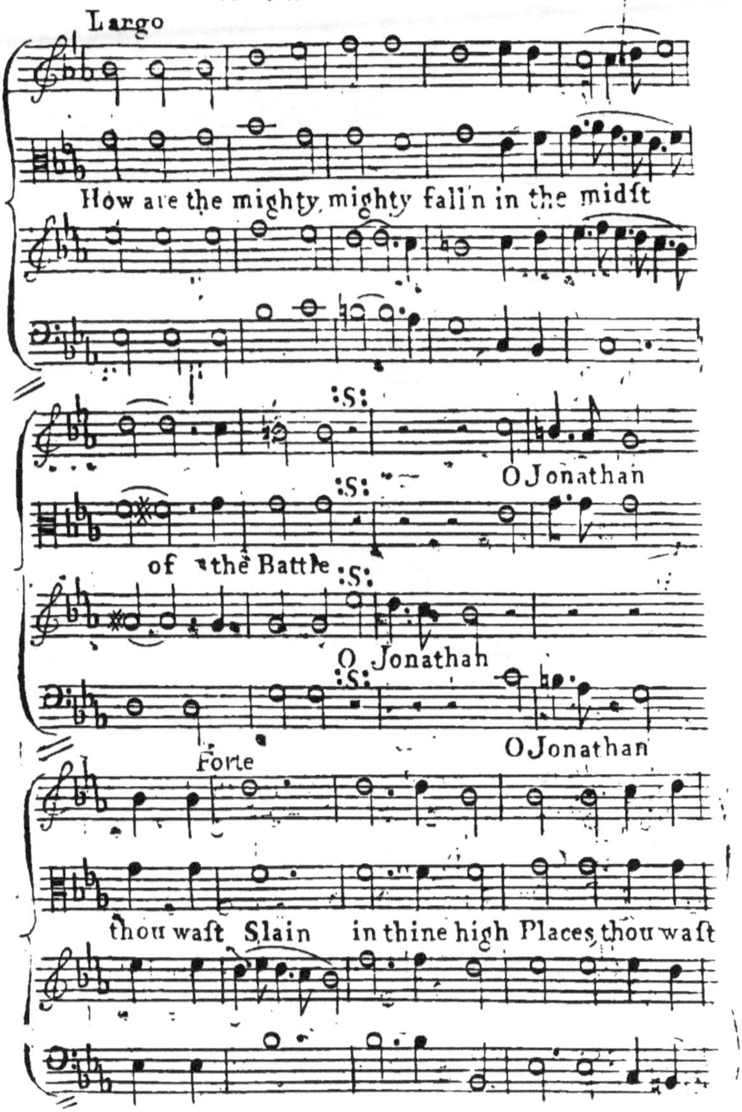
Largo
How are the mighty mighty fall'n in the midst
:S:
O Jonathan
of the Battle
O Jonathan
Forte
O Jonathan
thou wast Slain in thine high Places thou wast

www.ingramcontent.com/pod-product-compliance
Lightning Source LLC
Chambersburg PA
CBHW020925230426
43666CB00008B/1576